WANDERING OJAI

Poetry & Photographs

HOLLY WOOLSON

Copyright © 2020 by Holly Woolson
Wandering Ojai

Poetry & Photographs
by Holly Woolson

All rights reserved, including the reproduction
in whole or in part in any form
without the written consent of the author.

ISBN 978-0-578-76552-5

Book Design by Ojai Digital
ojaidigital.com
Ojai California

Published in the United States
by Tire Swing Studio
Ojai California

tireswingstudio.com

to Bruno,

my scruffy dog and loyal hiking companion

since 2007

Preface

In December 2018, my daughter gave me two books for Christmas, *Modern Japanese Tanka* (Makoto Ueda, 1996) and *Urban Tumbleweed, Notes from a Tanka Diary* (Harryette Mullen, 2013). I had never heard of tanka poetry, a centuries old form that follows the same syllabic pattern as Haiku with two additional lines at the end. Tanka poems have twenty-one syllables in total, usually organized in five lines of 5-7-5-7-7 syllables. To establish a regular writing routine, I set out to write an illustrated tanka poem everyday starting on the first of January 2019.

Over the course of the year, I regularly took tanka walks as described in Mullen's book. This practice of opening up to whatever inspiration might come my way was freeing and magical. Something always caught my attention and moved me to write, even when I felt distracted or stressed. With my phone in my pocket, I was able to take photographs of each inspiring encounter while constructing simple poems in my mind. When I got home, I wrote the poems down and posted them online, paired with a photograph. I only completed 159 poems that year, more than 200 fewer than I had hoped to write, but within that collection a rich dialogue emerged between me and this special place that I call home.

Ojai has a reputation as a highly spiritual spot. Along with its natural beauty, people talk about energy vortexes, the unique east-west orientation of the valley (only one of a half dozen on earth like it), and other mystical qualities that attract seekers from all over the world. Ojai has nurtured my spirit in profound ways too. By bringing me closer to nature and incorporating me into this eclectic community of compassionate residents, Ojai has coaxed me out of dark places, healed me, and challenged me at the same time.

For this collection I have carefully selected and edited twenty-four of the tanka poems that I wrote in 2019. I've organized them according to the four seasons of the year as a testament to my deep love for the rhythm of life in Ojai. They provide a glimpse into the wisdom that I have gained from my wanderings. Most of the poems are entitled with the names of places or trails where I ventured on my tanka walks with the hope that you, too, might go out and explore the wild beauty of this area. There are maps at the back of the book to orient you. If you open your heart and walk in silence, you may be surprised by what you discover.

Holly Woolson

SPRING

Saddle Trail

sprinkled with fresh dew
beneath morning sun and sky
tiny leaves unfurl
although branches are brittle
the mighty oak awakens

Sulphur Mountain Road

Anacapa Isle
riding on the horizon
like a humpback whale
the tumble of green land
zigzags toward your distant shore

Riverview Trailhead

shining strip of life
meandering to the sea
gone by tomorrow
carry away my sorrow
refresh my soul for today

Ventura River Preserve

leaves of bright grass green
spreading over hard ground
see the golden fields
an apt name for cheerful blooms
their innocence unlike mine

Fox Canyon Trail

imagination
is a bit like attention
opening new worlds
once I dreamed a sky garden
carpets of baby blue eyes

Casitas Pass Road

the second spring since
these hills were ravaged by fire
wildflowers cover
blackened branches, scorched remains
shouting gratitude for life

SUMMER

Rose Valley Falls

like a waterfall
my life pours through me
and unless I write
capturing it on the page
I'll explode or die from thirst

The Maricopa Highway

shedding hard black crust
they don a flowered mantle
steep mountainsides
turn into a tapestry
of majestic hope and strength

Parking Lot

burning black pavement
one hundred and one degrees
I dread each minute
until this damn heatwave breaks
why do I resist what is

Ojai Valley Trail

melancholy day
walking your length back and forth
while echoes of time
recall happy decades past
to join today's solitude

Ojai Avenue

the first of July
these chairs are a testament
convincing ourselves
that this safe small town is where
we can all claim shade for free

Bate's Beach

transformation stone
shoreline whittling away
from wind, sea, and time
until waves lie down on land
nature's sculpture at my feet

Moonset

the silver moon hung
above twilight's bright threshold
time creeping past me
earth groaning on its axis
peaks swallowing up the light

AUTUMN

Persimmon Hill

you silly humans
do not regret suffering
stand tall and branch out
be like us, whipped by the wind
reaching forever sunward

Wills Creek

like ruby red lips
luscious fruit of the wild rose
shines among dry brush
an offering to springtime
beauty persists to the end

Ventura River Rock

just hanging around
nothing to do but breathe
absorb the sunshine
help out some mutual friends
it's a simple lichen life

Will's Canyon Trail

bird toes, waffle soles
impressions in fine light soil
comings and goings
so many have passed this way
what tracks will I leave behind

Ojai Clock Tower

September twilight
crickets ceaselessly droning
filling up the night
like the ringing in my ears
when I refuse to listen

Signal Street

how Ojai does stuff
unapologetically
nature rules, cajoles
it's rustic, laid-back, charming
and rough around the edges

WINTER

Chief's Peak

Ojai December
ripening orange orchards
blankets of white snow
in the nest of my valley
my heart warms to winter's song

North Fulton Street

time is running out
we say don't waste a second
addicted to speed
we hurry through life but why
don't we keep our own sweet time

Toward Oso Ridge

Sophia, wisdom
fill me with your divine will
shine your light through me
though mortality divides
knit us together in love

Foothill Trail

wanting solitude
I climbed the high trail alone
met a stranger there
we rambled on together
got lost, came back, and were friends

Blue Skies

you simply go on
breathe, look around, live your life
clouds blow in and out
eternal blue skies beyond
trust what your eyes cannot see

Ojai Meadow Preserve

like crystal teardrops
bare January branches
drip with last night's rain
our parched land drinks her fill
our trees weeping for joy

MAPS

DOWNTOWN OJAI

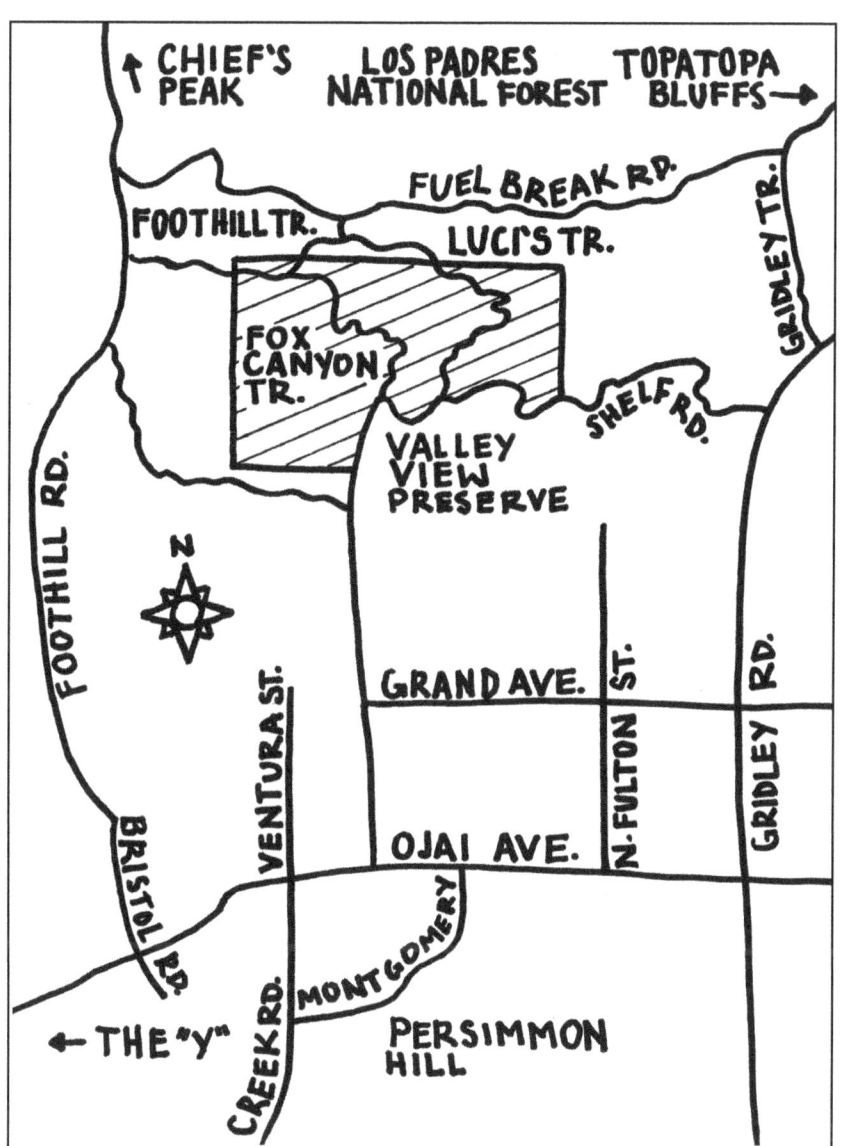

ENTERING OJAI

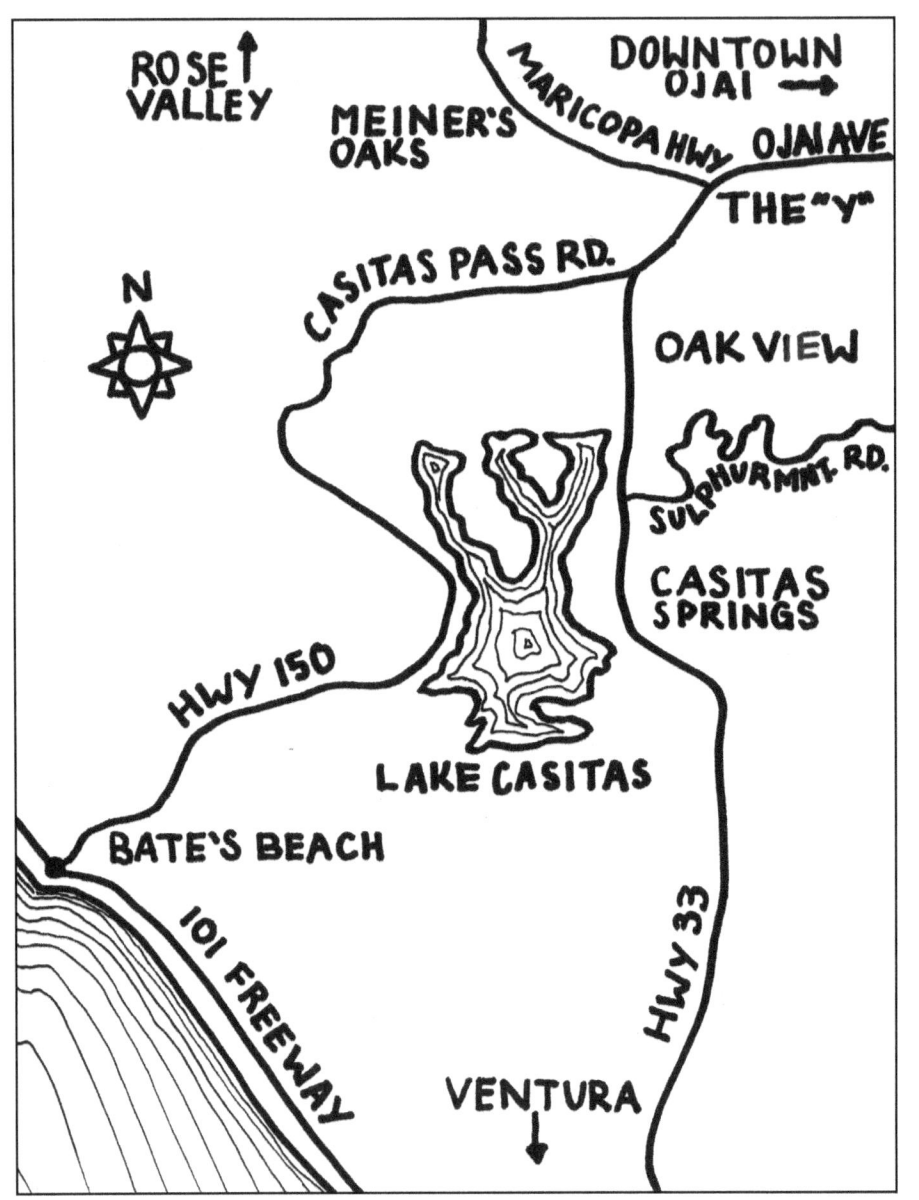

OJAI WEST

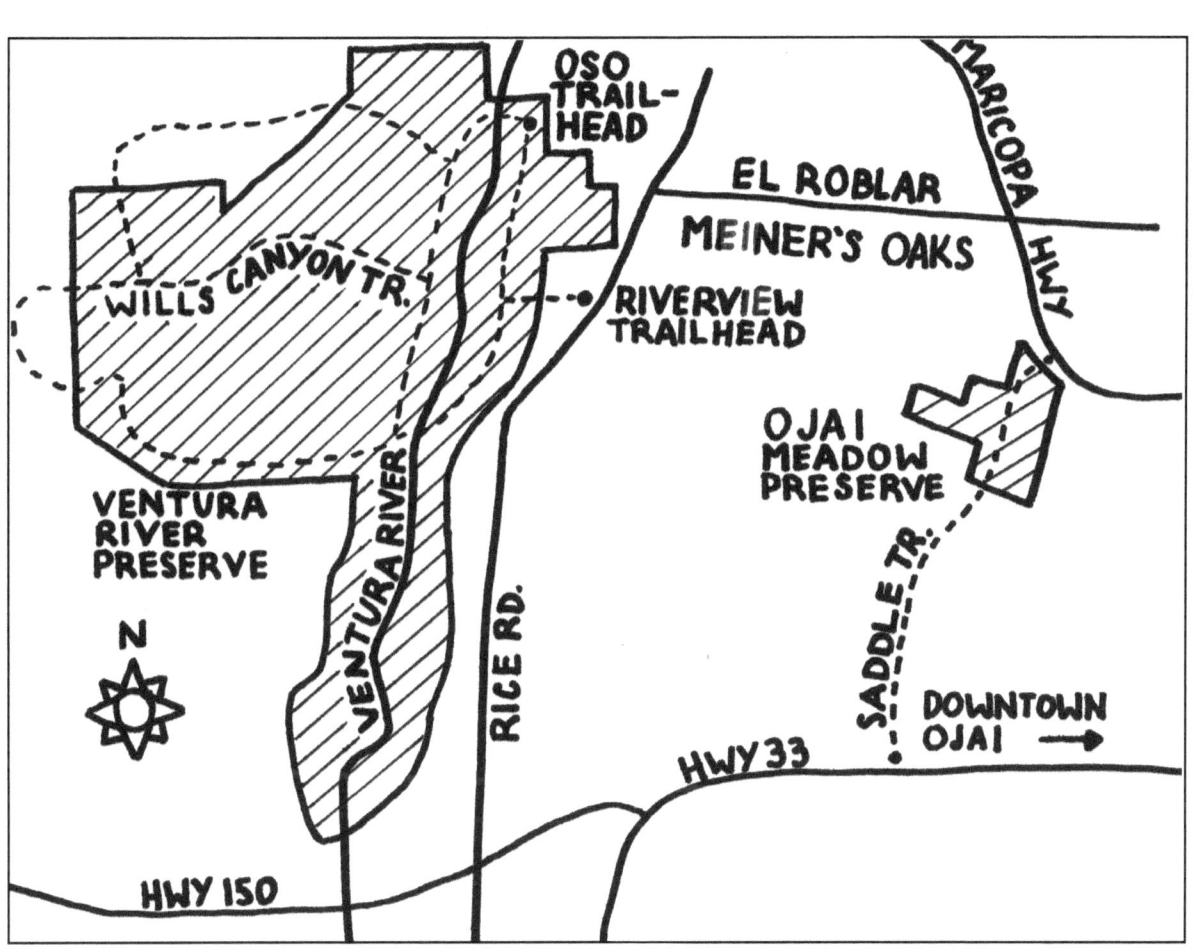

Acknowledgements

I am grateful to my family, friends, and fellow artists who accompany me on this journey through life, especially my daughter, Claire. Her thoughtfulness set me on a path that led to this book. She also contributed directly to this project by drawing the maps in the back. I also want to thank my artist friend Diana Smith for her encouragement and help. Finally, many thanks to my art teacher and friend, Amy Schneider. She gave me the skills and courage to create art again after a long hiatus. She also suggested the title and designed the layout for *Wandering Ojai*. Without her generosity, this project would not have come to fruition.

About the Author

Holly Woolson is an arts educator, painter, printmaker, photographer, and writer. She and her husband moved to Ojai in 1996 and raised their two children here. She currently works as the academic coordinator for a local non-profit organization, Art Trek Inc. *Wandering Ojai* is her first collection of poetry. Her next writing project, a memoir, tells the story of her adventures living in France when she was a young woman.

To learn more about Holly's work, please visit her website: www.tireswingstudio.com. Or visit Poppies Art and Gifts in downtown Ojai, an artists' cooperative gallery where Holly shows her work and teaches art classes. If you catch her while she's there, she will be happy to personally share with you her love of art and all things Ojai.

www.ingramcontent.com/pod-product-compliance
Lightning Source LLC
Chambersburg PA
CBHW061754290426
44108CB00029B/2990